SEASON
OF
MISSED CHANCES

PETER PEGNALL

Belfast
LAPWING

First Published by Lapwing Publications
c/o 1, Ballysillan Drive
Belfast BT14 8HQ
Lapwing.poetry@ntlworld.com
www.lapwingpoetry.com

British Library Cataloguing in Publication Data.
A catalogue record for this book is available from
the British Library.

Since before 1632
The Greig sept of the MacGregor Clan
Has been printing and binding books

All Lapwing Publications are
Printed and Hand-bound in Belfast
Set in Aldine 721 BT at the Winepress

ISBN 978-1-905425-95-2

CONTENTS

SEASON
OF
MISSED CHANCES

❖

PETER PEGNALL

To
Eliza,
my daughter

SEASON OF MISSED CHANCES

Like the time my plasticine garden
won third prize in the wolf cubs' jamboree,
despite the pink daisies. Or Carol's face,
framed in the Inter-City One Two Five,
her curled wave and that final cadence:
'I always preferred Robin, you know.'
There was a hazy mist in York Station that night.

Like those long three months as scorched leaves tumbled,
as my father shrivelled into a man
who couldn't care. Sealed in the back bedroom,
we might have raked the lawn in our minds,
taken Agincourt. Instead, I allowed
domestic police to cordon the zone.
Nothing can be so wrong not to talk about.

And now, as Virginia Creeper
blushes strawberry, as schoolchildren scamper
or dawdle, as bonfires bless the evening air,
as my fourth four flat dreams a fire place
and roast chestnuts disappoint again,
I do not sit at the desk, smudge the page,

spider a poem to net myself in a drop of dew.

FAREWELLS I

F.W.WOOLWORTH

I'd buy my mum 'April Violets'
drop my school cap on plastic soldiers,
nick them.
      Once, I splintered a stink bomb in the store
gazed in glee as shoppers gagged and fled.

A time of pocket money and easy theft,
rubbish covers of rubbish songs,
winceyette and fablon, sherbet lemons,
sweet sixteen year olds, chewing gum.

When they closed down,
hordes queued for pink dolls,
electronic potato slicers. Nostalgia

was not on sale. Their best item.

FAREWELLS II

HAROLD PINTER

Wait for it.

This man gained eloquence by leaving things out:

you would not go to his birthday party.
Something baroque in those truncated
monologues. Something rich in poverty.
His gritty voice cornered his characters:

a clockwork key in their rigid bodies.

I saw him once in the Café Royal,
next to Antonia. Two gorgeous,
silent, flightless songbirds in mourning.

FAREWELLS III

TO STEVEN CLAYTON,
who escaped with cuts and bruises

They didn't get much done those lunchtimes,
two crumpled cherubs in their cups,
middle-aged playmates, devoted to folly
and staying out. On the zigzag journey home
keys, wallets, mobile phones sprayed across the streets,
as the evening softened into forget.

Forget and forge into another day,
linen shirts swirl in dandy pretence,
as perfectly poached eggs smile like small suns.
Why stride back towards that darkened back room,
sparkled with vodka wit and claret friendship?

They weren't in it for the razzmatazz,
or the small town celebrity. Relished
sweet canters of gossip and ebullience,
spied each new shape in the doorway with glee,
with ill-concealed derision. This stage play world
held for a time; solitude had the last word.

FAREWELLS IV

FATHERS

You see that figure on the country road?
he has a long way to go, past guardsmen poplars,
past poppy fields, past grey horses in meadows.
going nowhere, but going on...

This is a comfort, I don't know why:
know even less why I cannot speak with him.
What were the words we shared in those lost years?

As a tree grows older, it grows stronger
as a river matures it flows crazy
as a man ripens, he rots.

But I don't believe he's gone. Last night
he nudged me with a smile, made tea and biscuits,
taught me the names of wild flowers,
flung aside the blanket that smothered both of us.

She was not to blame; her black cloud lingers;
little to read in that sad mystery.

Nick, you forage for sideways tracks, cry
like a snowy owl. I enjoy walking beside you,
scan the horizon for signs of life...

Death is another matter.

FAREWELLS V

AN OLDER MAN IN A RICHMOND PATISSERIE

Thank you for the loan of the biro.
It's enough to know you touched the plastic,
I loved the shrug that said it didn't matter,
I might have kept it.
            didn't want to;
fancied one more word before you
served cakes and coffee
            to the coven of mums
who swapped speeches of child-care and Provence,
divorce settlements and Reiki healing.

Solitude, your biro, your lovely, tired eyes:
what a feast, as I say, happily, goodbye.

THE OUTLINE OF HILLS

Held us in its palm while we brewed dissent,
past the bluebells, past the tumbledown mill.

High on the other side of the valley,
Lumb Bank. Couldn't say we fought like racoons,
or even jackdaws. Just being caged.
Love smothers and starves, like earth under earth.

If you look over towards Haworth, you'll glimpse
a funnel of light. Over there. Not here.

BANK HOLIDAY ROMANCE

It might have been war-time; cheek by jowl
in a carriage on platform seventeen.
No information. 'Incident at Clapham.'
Men in uniform walk away as we speak.
Chelsea fans sober up, ebb into wise-crack,
menacing as scones and tea at Aunt Emma's.

Still we wait. Splutters of engine,
doors wheeze entry to one more inmate,
resented.

At last! 'The replacement driver's on his way.'
Lies breed like plankton, we drown slowly,
mingle rueful glances.
                    Then, with no warning,
a breeze of love. Canon Julius Raindrop
swishes aside his cassock, spears
heartsick Edna with a matador's flourish.
Trev and Robbie rise together, glad and shy,
crushed cans of Stella their private confetti.
Something happens in the toilet, three times:
that last minute at *Simply Food*
came in handy.
                    And everywhere, discarded lace,
angles to grace a tantric master,
suave economy of movement,
greasy passages.

Movement of another kind, as the guard,
crouched in his cage, stutters apologies
and it's *Westward Ho!* for Clapham Junction.

The same again, never the same again,
it might have been war-time, we wear our secrets
with pride. Redress our small realities,
as if Christ had made a station stop,
gorged on Burger King at Waterloo.

You don't believe a word of this, do you?

HOPE FOR BREAKFAST

Let me invite you to my friend's kitchen.

There's a bottle of Famous Grouse
            next to last night's beetroot sandwich,
half gnawed.

Radio 4 blabbers on about
the decline of this and that,
the long march of the Emperor Penguin,
the fate of the apostrophe;
combative churls winkle away
at slippery sods or bemused experts.
But he does not switch it off
because he cannot switch himself off.

★

Somewhere an eight month old child
            reaches towards the early light
smiles like an opened daisy.

Some time at some time in some lives
            there was hope for breakfast.

'WHEN I PLAY CHOPIN,
THE PIANO BECOMES A MAGIC GARDEN'
(Artur Rubinstein)

My granddaughter flaps her arms and flies,
she becomes the swallows above her curly head;
all her dreams are real. Something tears at me
however weird and hopeful I've managed
to remain. Tainted by the Circle Line,
it's never been easy to live for now.

My brother speaks like a Gatling gun,
knows everything from Wittgenstein's inside leg
to the pink elephant in the phone box,
has a private line to the archangels.
When his fingers caress a nocturne on the keys,
he sits still, the best place he's ever been.

It is wonderful to kneel on the earth,
marigolds and pansies cupped in our palms.
To give something back to where we shall return,
to smile for no reason, beyond reason,
to wait for what cannot be imagined.

ON THE OTHER SIDE

When Oscar set his size twelves on the quayside,
did he expect a fanfare of pipes,
a garland of blushing young matelots?
The very least, a seat at the round table,
prince of *Des Tribunaux*, scourge of hypocrite,
skinflint, sycophant, the second-rate.

Beardsley and Blanche passed by on the other side,
cold shouldered his salute.
       And so to Berneval,
redolent and exotic as Newhaven.
Where to fly next? 'De Profundis, the Sequel'?

As usual, safer to return to sorrow,
squander every last tissue of credit,
imagine golden days that weren't there.
'The worst inn's worst room welcomes Mr Wilde.'
       Even the wall paper peeled away.

NICO
I have no regrets, except, perhaps, that I was born a woman

A cellar bar, Moss Side, Manchester:
she looms through the yellow smoke, bloated, haggard
'Has anyone seen my black cloak?'
Something clicks,
a fainter shade of skeletal beauty,
that barbed wire voice. Then, with a whisper of grace,
she's gone. Leaves snapshots of the sixties,
our own Chelsea Girls, exploding plastic nights.

She was tone deaf, acted like a mannequin,
conspired her own iconography.
Even now, there are stony acolytes,
grim reapers in suburban sitting rooms,
glutted on gothic monosyllables.

The mirror cracked, Sunday crawled through the week;
think of superstardom with your legs apart
think of Lou Reed, Jim Morrison, Dylan
scored on your wrist.
      Think what it must be like
to be every one's sex machine, no-one's wife,
a relic on a hundred thousand shelves.

OH, HER SKIRT IT SWAYED AS THE GUITAR PLAYED...

These sunflowers marched from Silves
to Santander, spent a rowdy night
in Plymouth, all sailors and easy women;
took a slow train to Waterloo,
shivered on the station, as newspapers
announced slumps in retail, Britney's re-birth,
some judge in high heels and suspenders,
another spat between super-chefs.

They arrived by the silver Thames,
on a golden, golden day,
on a breath of wind.

They came here, and here they'll stay
until bin men cart them away.

ASSAULT
written after an attack in Twickenham

They won't forget me in a hurry. What a dent
my skull made in his boot. And what about my gibe,
that mordant, icy: 'I feel sorry for you.'?

A blood-sick tide rages and roars,
   iron bars squeeze and batter my brow,
the pillow's sodden, a shape lurks
   behind the blinds.
Again to tumble and crash
   screech and cackle like a spectre
as friendly hands reach out,
flail and grasp only air.

And now I start when push-chairs converge,
when someone darts too close behind,
when there's an echo in the alleyway.

   Let us be kind
to one another, if not kind
courteous, if not courteous
tolerant, amiable, decent,
forgiving, forgiving.
   I feel sorry for you,
whose life is violence, vacancy, noise.

I shall, it seems, recover.

WRITE ME DOWN

A strange fairy landed in my hotel room,
danced across the frayed carpet, spangled stars
in a dank afternoon. Hid in the wardrobe,
tunnelled under the bed-clothes, chomped custard creams,
tied knots in my hair as we devoured stories,
hatched secret plans, shooed away monsters,
sang 'Puff the Magic Dragon' in our own land,
our own frolicked seaside, our own Honalee.

'Write me down,' she cried, as she skipped and flew,
as she packed the moment with real dreams,
scintillations. 'Write me down, Grandpa,
then I shall always be this way, beside you,
two silly-billies in a cast iron world.'

So here are some modest words to write you down,
beyond belief, comfortable, exotic,
rainbow streaks in a bubble of love.

DON'T LEAVE ME NOW
a long way after Jacques Brel

Must I forget these hours between us?
Wear our love like a cross?

Don't leave me now
Shall I speak slimy words
Or croon like a cow
Stranded in mud and turds?

Why should I recall your dance
The fear of your tears
The shadow of your hand, your name
The story, the dreams
The blush, the scarlet and black

I want you back

SHAME

Gnaws to the bone,
        worse when you don't know
                what you've gone and done now.

A hooded crow
        gorges on mistake
after mistake. Oh no —
you blabbed, a freak of hot air,
        puppet of self-pity:
'Love me. Love me until I break.'

No ready ointment
        no forgiving spark;
guilt, the master spiv
        mugs your spirit

                indwells your precious lives.

IO NON V'INVIDIO PUNTO, ANGELI SANTI
For Edith Lillian Westbrook and Susanna Maria Nash

I don't envy you in the least, Holy Angels;
serenity palls: me for the switchback,
the gulp. Without deep night, no glistering frost
no Milky Way. Engulf your forever,
leave me down here, among the spindrift leaves.

Imagine exhaustion. Imagine sweet peace.
I saw this in grandma's glittering eyes
that night she swanned away. She breathed life
as she breathed her last, glimpsed buttered bread, tea,
that cushioned warmth the drugs had all but drained:
imagine.

This Easter, Susanna's birthday, two years old,
rascal of the rock pools, goofy oddment,
seamstress of these ragged, patchwork days,
each urgent, almost-sentence a hymn of praise.

KIP

A guest house by the Thames, mildewed window frames,
scratches and scuffles in the alleyway.
Iron bedsteads. Keep my wallet under the pillow,
sweat fever on the brown sheets. These are my friends:
Willie, saw active service in Aden
sees it again every night. Strokes his kilt
as you might stroke a kitten, jerks and squints,
has been writing home for twenty years, unsent.
Jonjo sat in on a session with Hendrix,
that creased photograph passport to a smoke,
a pint. His hair doesn't quite know what to do,
he's a voodoo chile in Oxfam denims,
sometimes a study in marble tenderness.
We've all been inside, learnt to be alone
in the stink of too many... I was —
but never mind. Daily I am expecting.
She would be thirty five by now. A woman.
Somewhere she moves through a soft morning.

PRAYER FOR A COMMONWEALTH,
REMEMBRANCE DAY 2007.

When the snow melted, the River Aire ran red;
hacked torsos in ditches and stubble fields,
limbs manured the spring cabbage, decked the gorse.
Brothers lay spread-eagled, like love gone wrong.

Now it's all long-distance firework nights,
play station desert storms, push button
genocide. There are wars and there are roses
and there are tribes at each other's throats
as the last sulphur sizzles, suffocates.

This morning, two doves perched on my washing line.
I kept my silence. There may yet be time.

POLSKI SKLEP

A gentle summer afternoon;
tables on the pavement,
bottles of Brok Export. For once
they talk to each other, don't bark at the phone.
The man on the left seems to have grown
a slug on his upper lip.

Clustered, angular, persevering,
they might slide down the High Street
through the red light, past Macdonald's
past another shuttered music shop.

Miles from home cash sings in their pockets
spills into rare smiles, return tickets.

RED RIDING HOOD'S SIDE OF THE STORY
for Antonia and Elena

To be honest, I rather liked the wolf;
I'd been fed up to the back teeth,
being little Miss Nice. My granny
smelt a bit and my mum only gave me grief.

Imagine spending half term holiday
trailing through the forest like a servant,
laden with cake and elderberry wine;
Wolfie's smirk and silky words were divine.

So, no thanks, woodchopper, cut your own logs
and no thanks fairy tales, they're for the dogs.
I'm happier here with my ruffian friend
munching and slurping until springtime ends.

FOR THE CHILDREN AT
THE VICARAGE SCHOOL

I think I saw a thousand stars
they rested here
they were eyes
glistered like beads of blackberry
questioned like the long night.

They said' look at me, I'm little'
they said, 'I love ice cream,
my scatty spaniel, my dizzy sister
my dreams, my picnic dreams.'

They said to me 'don't be dull,
like a ditch where watercress grow
like a long lesson when
the arithmetic bird
gouges your neck
or someone else
knows the answer
to some silly question
that only some fool would want to know.'

Those eyes said to me
that we only had
the gorgeous joy,
the current moment, the chocolate taste
of tomorrow.

Their eyes said to me,
that they were holy lambs of god
and that one day,
when the moorhen wind themselves
towards the river bank,

when the apples tumble fat and juicy
from the humble trees
when the toad sings like the lark
and having fun is free

then, and only then,
is Jerusalem here, in our hearts
the Vicarage an open, unfee'd door.

CHA

In Pakistan tea is called love.
They take it daily, a gift from above,
Or rather down below, in the soil.
It is more precious than gold, or oil.

TWO IN A BUS SHELTER IN TWICKENHAM

Take away Prawn Chow Mein with plastic spoons:
this slewed couple dipped into glutamate,
chewed soggy noodles as the rain called the tune,
the bus didn't arrive. He, bald as an egret,
she, dumpy in tartan. They have their secrets:
his mother in Newport Pagnell, her chocolate.
So far, they have not touched, have not dared;
only utensil clacked with utensil.

This bus stop could be an anywhere,
a beach bar in Copacabana, a cell,
a roller coaster ride in war-time Blackpool.
For now, plastic is silver, Prawn Chow Mein
Lobster Thermidor. In that rain, like wine.

ANGEL

You're a sixties chick, Susie. As Mick drawled,
Jimi snarled through smoky Soho basements,
as Terence Stamp dished cool love to us all,
did you flaunt Biba beauty? Smooch in a tent?

We are still here, bright singed butterflies,
volumes of delayed hope. Don't ask why,
as long as blueberry ice cream on apple pie
trickles down the gullet. Now please don't cry,

sweet Susie. There are reasons for tears,
there are moments when short winter days
last hours too long. When it seems that lies
march like commandoes through hymns of praise.

At The Ritz, Terence Stamp still sips lemon tea,
chomps anchovy toast. And there is you,
wild as a tree, glamorous as regret.

FORBIDDEN FRUIT

That summer season, when slender legs
sprout in Hyde Park, when Uncle Trevor dons shorts,
when there's a fizz in the cool larder of your heart,
when you drain each crystal goblet to the dregs...
when you cannot finish a sentence you did not start.

This summer I shall write the novella
other men can only envy. Jam packed,
elegant, trenchant, a silk umbrella
butterflied over a sun-burnt soul...
                    I've got it cracked.

NO EDWARD HOPPERS IN HOUNSLOW
The Day Room

We're not nighthawks, more like stuffed parrots
or scrawny pigeons. Except we've given up the
the squawk, we're unlikely to scavenge
or shit on statues of eminent men.

Graced by a brown sofa, the lounge stinks of fags,
worships Bargain Hunt and Jeremy Kyle.
There is a woman who rocks, sports dark glasses
in the half-light, reads her fortune in cold tea.

Len hides a flask to stoke his purple cheeks,
his blueberry veins. Brown paper crinkles,
he shakes less, then more, then less again, then more;
that smile is a cornered mongrel.

There are three bachelors of art, a midwife,
one conviction for improper behaviour,
an equity card (circa nineteen sixty).
Hope is a dead letter, though now and then
memories barge into the trenchant silence:

'I gave her everything, what more could she want?'

'My son's coming to take me home tonight,
he's had it with these so-called doctors.
Doesn't suffer fools gladly, my Tony.
Busy man. Not too busy for his old mum.'

Forgive us for wearing stereotypes
like slippers. It's the torpor that drains
as we drain away and look forward
to what's around the corner, the next dose.

WINTERING IN

There are days the lights stay out. Days you lurk,
sitting room, tea and biscuit, closed curtain days.
As if the television were your only friend,
the answer-phone a drawer bridge. Days you stoke
embers in a guttering heart, make no plans,
glow with the small gratitude of being here,
the terrified relief that it's over. Soon.

Then, taken by ambush, icy sunlight,
tomorrow invites you to the party,
no more secrets, no more blessed solitude,
garrulous as a capuchin monkey,
you bare your arse to an unamazed world.
If that's all you had to show, better to stay
indoors, dictate your memories to the moon,
the visiting moon.

POEMS SUGGESTED BY PHRASES FROM
SCOTT FITZGERALD'S 'TENDER IS THE NIGHT'

A Scherzo of Colour

Bougainvillea against a plaster wail,
pink lips parted in desire;
a pool of blood in the doorway.

Lap it all up.

If you prefer black and white,
        a touch of evil –
fly a dark kite
        hieroglyph of agony.

A Carnival of Affection

They all come to the party –
Little Noddy and Wittgenstein
Winston Churchill and Gary Glitter

And isn't that Audrey Hepburn
arm in arm with
      F. Scott Fitzgerald?
The host went to bed early, alone,

smoked salmon
smeared on the ormolu mirror.

A chord of delight

Plunk.
That's how his fingers struck the mandolin:
he'd half expected to satisfy
        half the female congregation,

section the other half.

"You're 'avin a laugh, boy,
you wouldn't know a tune
        from your epiglottis..."

Nevertheless, once in a while,
an accord of delight –
she said, quietly, she might

A Hard Boiled Sparkle in His Eyes

Not how she'd imagined breakfast.
They were mute.
        His opened broadsheet
a River Lethe between them.

'Had you forgotten?' she didn't say.

        Served her right.

Cooked to a turn in Veuve Cliquot

Reality is not what it was
        for the Widow Cliquot:
there is rust in the geranium,
        a nervous tic in the Venetian blind.

Best get slewed, trip
        the light fantastic,

crunch the meringue,
        raise our tulip flutes
            and rejoice.

BRIGHT SCARF

Guy de Vol au Vent, Belgian poet,
draped a woolly scarf on a snowman.
Waited, stately in a homburg,
until his tearful friend entered the earth;
a scarlet ribbon festooned the sludge.

When it's darker outside than in,
when the milk's just slightly turned,
when all the envelopes are windowed,
when you'd sooner not do what you're doing.
Wear it. Strut like a peacock on the high street,
fool yourself into fooling others,
follow the flag, whistle as you go-go.

My mum knitted this new one,
her eyes aren't what they were,
but it's snazzy and cool,
perfectly imperfect.
        It says I'm proud of her
        it says I'm still a map of mischief
it says *don't mess with my tribe*:

us wild ones who live over and over,
pirates on a lily pond, Bright Scarves.

DECEMBER, 1969
For Brian Binding and Tom Brunsden, with love

That Friday evening, the snow swept across Richmond,
cars in the high street slewed onto the pavement,
The town froze to a halt, swathed in beauty.
Tom and I dragged the sledge towards the hill,
our faces taut with icy smiles, noses
cherry red, glad to take time out of time.

We sped and tumbled, two secret agents
in bobble hats, our mission to save the world
by having fun. On our third trip, we met Brian,
a small man drowned in a cashmere coat,
teacher magician, bundle of wit and warmth;
there was a coal fire in his flat, cocoa,
a splash of brandy, crumpets and butter,
Archangelo Corelli's Christmas concerto,
a hint of the illicit in our eyes.

Amazed as the Magi, we worshipped
without prayer; a nine year old boy, a teenage
drifter, a man who knew how to live alone:
all three changed, the same, safe in the darkened night.

SKINT IN HARROD'S FOOD HALL

Fantails of perch and bream
primeval squabbles of lobster
prawns wink in aspic.

There's the walrus, glass in paw
slurps oysters with his sad friend
sings of his whiskered greed.

Over there, tongues curl in silence
porkers grin, sides of beef drip blood,
guinea fowl and canard nestle close.

And cheese and artichoke
and Chateau Lafitte
other things sweet but I'm a bloke.

"Can I help you, sir?"
"Yes, please. Do you take..."
"Don't concern yourself with payment, sir.
I'd never forget a face like yours. Would
you mind signing this for my daughter?"

Luckily I didn't have a pen.
Luckily I ran out
luckily I recalled better days
luckily my inner resources.

Pass the ketchup.

FREEDOM PASS

There's a man on the bus wields a golf club:
it's his way into story time. Tournaments
he'd won, or nearly won. Troon. Royal Portrush.
Invercockieleekie. Once, in Las Vegas
how he'd trounced Dean 'Bottles' Martin,
how they'd sauced in a pool of Jack Daniels.
How Sinatra sang
                so tenderly, so casually,
about a man who shouldered a guitar
                but couldn't play
about a lover glued to a photograph
                a weightlifter with no arms.

And how Deano paid the bill
                Bollinger breakfasts and all
and told him, between brilliantine and tears
                to call.

For now, the man on the bus
                exploits his freedom pass to the full
transports his mashie from Feltham to Chiswick
                limpets himself to the nearest ear
and, when he's cleared the seats around him
chirrups 'I diddle diddle I do
Diddle I do do do.'

As if he were back in Limerick
        marooned with his drained mother
her knitting needles clacking out the life
she hoped he'd venture.

Or there, in Kilburn, on a steel bed frame
sealing ten pounds a week and wild nights
in a rumpled envelope;
        as yet, no grandchildren.

As we skim past Twickenham Green, he smiles:
        something he's never done wells in his eyes.

OUR JOB IS TO MAKE MUSIC
WITH WHAT REMAINS

Jim was blind, flung his head back like a seal,
barked laughter in his cavern of lanterns;
fascinated, clueless, unsure, I'd cling close,
marvel at his twiglet fingers on the keys.

What was this world, why did these sounds thrill,
appal, drain? How he fluted his lips over tea,
how his pupils rolled back, how his pimpled neck
bulged from a well ironed shirt,
fed a kind of guilt.
Never such courage, not for the boy
who whimpered for a light in the hallway,
who gathered scarecrows with machine guns
round his bedside.
Jim played on. Chopin,
Gershwin, Debussy. Chomped his fish paste sandwich
with lip-smacking gusto. Made his own way home.

Because there is no choice.
Because we can do it.
Because there is a cacophony of alone.
Because we grind out years
          waiting for that voice.

Broken bones, broken guitar strings
      broken promises;
families broken, gushed away:
      an uncivil war.

Rose-Bay Willow Herb
      amongst the jagged bricks:
this stage-set devastation
      sky line like broken teeth.

      For those who who are lost, make music,
for those yet to come, make music
      for those who curse, crush or maim,
          make music that will remain.

UNDER THE WAVES

You can't keep the sea out of things;
did you cry and curl up your feet the first time,
or hurtle like clockwork towards the foam?
The water's warm in the rock pools, small crabs
scuttle under speckled rocks. Gazing out,
you can't tell the sky from the sea,
fasten on distant yachts, the pale winter sun.

She walked ahead, it seemed like sure of herself;
skipped a little, waded up to her knees,
cut her shape into the shoreline.
Did I break in? Or play at solitude?
we go back, go back, forget what we found.

This is the world. It's full of adventure.
there are gazelles in Africa, strangers
next door. Like gods we invade the sky, kill
time as if we lived forever. I want
treasures you can't touch, an innocent eye.
I don't mind walking by the sea, for now.

Dancing on the surface,
        like you dance along the sea-bed:
brilliant, trembling, weightless
        dead and alive. Like yesterday.
But who you are claws you back
into being nice, being half-here
calling for disappointment,
like a child who runs behind the gang,
won't stop, even bent double with stitch.

Why must I tell the same story,
see the same frantic faces
mouthing?
No further forward than a pendulum,
slicing close to my heart. Why bother
when the ones you love are the ones you fail?
Or that's what they tell you in so many words.

The place you can't escape, the fears you can't face,
the night that's always 4 a.m.
something happened, then, something you repeat
and never get right. Would it help to know?

Make a list of how you'll spend the next day:
answer letters, write reviews, telephone
friends in need. Exhaust yourself then wonder
how it all went; imagine open space,
the cormorant's screech, fingers lightly touching, sighs
like surging water, breath like springtime breeze
bodies falling and rising together,
together. Don't ask why it has to end.

Don't let it end.
Live knowing you'll leave
and that love whispers like a sea-shell
in all the places you'll never call home.

VOTIVE

There's a sacred grove in the Royal Park;
stags trail bracken and dry grass in their antlers,
square up to each other, scrape the sandy earth.

Like ballerinas the does tiptoe and bend,
their beauty as real and fleeting as autumn,
camouflaged in ancient oak, plump chestnut.

No wonder the gods kept warm in their hides,
small men arced arrows and called themselves kings,
threw the guts and entrails to sleek hounds.

Squirrels crunch acorns in their praying paws,
honour the circle we can only break –
so we stand far, inhale suspension of time.

Susanna, your hungry eyes eat up
the unending envelope of your world
your amazement itself a mystery.

Don't lose what you bring to each bright moment –
a smile that slices through granite, through gloom.
You are there, in that magic circle. Stay.

GOING HOME

There are many ways to reach where we have to go;
a fox skips between garbage can and the undergrowth;
a teenager casually reaches for another pot noodle
Charlie Parker soared like a buzzard over Arizona.

My way is in the sand, by the marram grass;
in the kitchen, sea bream steams in wild herbs and lemon,
inside a poem by William Blake.

With my hand in my granddaughter's hand
Hope lives until it's time to go where I have to go.

Peter Pegnall